The Wedding
Photographer's Handbook

The Wedding Photographer's Handbook

◆

a guide
to modern wedding photography

Gene Ho

iUniverse, Inc.

New York Lincoln Shanghai

The Wedding Photographer's Handbook
a guide to modern wedding photography

Copyright © 2007 by Gene Ho

iUniverse books may be ordered through booksellers or by contacting:

iUniverse
2021 Pine Lake Road, Suite 100
Lincoln, NE 68512
www.iuniverse.com
1-800-Authors (1-800-288-4677)

ISBN: 978-0-595-44228-7 (pbk)
ISBN: 978-0-595-88559-6 (ebk)

Printed in the United States of America

Special Thanks

Melissa Driggers Lemmons
Nadean Bruehlman
Emily Massingill

To my mother. Who taught me about responsibility, life and the meaning of family.

Contents

Forward

by *Melissa Driggers Lemmons—MBA*

When I was first asked to write about Gene Ho, the thing that came to my mind was leadership. But when I started interviewing his photographers, I found out that none of them viewed Gene as a leader. In fact, even Gene doesn't view himself as a leader.

A leader can be defined by many things, or possess many different characteristics. In my opinion, what matters most is not how a dictionary defines a leader, but how each individual defines what they believe makes a leader.

Gene Ho Photography has been operating successfully for seventeen years in Myrtle Beach, SC. The business has grown so much that he now has twenty photographers in his company and is now operating in six cities: Atlanta, Charleston, Savannah, Reno, Wilmington, and Myrtle Beach. Gene Ho has come to be known as one of the best photographers in the business.

Gene was born in Brooklyn, New York, and is a first generation American from Chinese immigrants who legally came into the United States from Hong Kong and Malaysia. Gene eventually relocated to Myrtle Beach to attend Coastal Carolina University for a short period. He discovered his calling after his first amateur photo shoot, which was one of his first homework assignments for a freshman photography class. He had found his niche.

In order to be a successful photographer, you do not have to have a million degrees or be certified in any way. You just have to possess the ability and the know-how. Gene constantly looks for ways to improve or to see things in a different light. He does this by studying biographies. He studies how great men in our past have dealt with creating things out of nothing. They are not necessarily men of photography. Gene chooses to learn from people who have succeeded in their own realm. For example, he studies Jesus, Napoleon, Job, Sun Tzu, and Alexander the Great.

Gene is not only a photographer, but he is a teacher as well. He is the Director of Photography at Horry-Georgetown Technical College. He also holds private workshops and occasionally speaks at other colleges. He is able to share his gift and talent with others who share his same interests and help them to succeed.

My definition of leadership philosophy is to simply believe in yourself, and believe you can help others to succeed. But it was very interesting getting responses from Gene and his colleagues because I found that none of them saw Gene as a leader! Perhaps it is just view leadership differently. Maybe they adopt Gene's thinking on leadership. Gene's philosophy is, "Follow me because I'm heading in the same direction as you."

To get a better understanding of Gene Ho, I chose to give a survey to a few of his photographers. One interesting comment was from Nadean Bruehlman, one of his lead photographers and office manager. According to the wise words of her grandpa, she said, "No man can demand respect, you have to earn it." What she respects about Gene is that he knows where he is weak and he also understands to get outside help when he is not the best person for the job.

Through my interviews, I find that even though Gene many not see himself as a leader, he is in fact one. He knows where he is going and says follow me if you want to come.

So … follow along.

Why Weddings

I love weddings.

To be honest … they are my first choice of what I like to photograph.

The reason is that I like to capture emotion.

Granted—you can find that in other things.

But there is nothing like weddings.

There's an amazing thrill in being in the center of all the excitement every week.

But if you find yourself not being particularly drawn to doing wedding … there another compelling reason for learning to do them.

Weddings are the road to photographic freedom.

Let me explain.

Economically, weddings ground you.

Weddings are the road to your personal artistic freedom.

It gives you the freedom to do anything you want … Monday through Friday.

For example … I love shooting portfolios.

For the past few years … I've been taking pictures for the Atlanta Falcon Cheerleaders.

That is a great job. I get to photograph beautiful women.

I've photographed their team pictures … I've shot their swimsuit calendar.

And the girls also call me up when they need their personal modeling portfolios shot.

Now let's imagine this same scenario if I WASN'T doing weddings.

Let's see ...

The swimsuit calendar took 5 working days to shoot. The digital work on it took about 3 days. Then you have to calculate in the time going back and forth to get pictures approved.

All said and done ... we're looking at 10 days of work.

At a "just get by" quote—you charge a $100 a day. And that is CHEAP!!!

$100 a day x 5 days a week x 50 weeks a year is $25,000.

That's your "just get by" quote.

So your minimum quote is $1,000 for the job.

Realistically ... you would need to charge at least $300 a day to be remotely profitable. (Not to mention to get what you're worth.)

So a 5-day Calendar shoot (which in reality is a 10-day job after editing, digital darkroom work and so-forth)—should be invoiced out at $3,000.

Now ... if I'm NOT doing weddings ... I send them a proposal to do the shoot for $3,000.

But here's the thing ...

Management at the Atlanta Falcons knows what they are doing.

At that level ... most organizations are willing to pay top dollar for quality work.

But they also know that the relationship is mutual. An Atlanta Falcon's photo shoot on your resume is priceless.

So no matter how great and wonderful you are as a photographer ... $3,000 is a tall order.

But here's the thing …

In the 10-day stretch, let's say that you have two weddings that are approximately $3,000 or so in your pocket.

So … you not only get to be more reasonable in your proposal … but you don't even have quote "going rates."

What sounds better to a big organization like the Falcons?

$3,000 for the shoot or:

$800 cash … Four tickets to the Dallas game … and a free ad in the Falcon's yearbook.

Believe me … the latter is much more appealing to any company.

With weddings, you can be extremely competitive.

Without the wedding you have to work so much harder to get your jobs.

Think of weddings as your ticket to personal freedom.

Granted … I love shooting weddings.

But even if I hated them … I know it would be what I HAD to do to make it as a photographer.

With weddings … I can pick and choose my M-F photo jobs.

I could even pick and choose what I wanted to shoot.

Without weddings, I would be a very difficult person to deal with.

I would have to make sure that all my photo shoots were profitable.

I would have to make sure that all assignments would bring in the overall dollars.

If had a chance to shoot the Atlanta Falcons for $800 or a real estate convention that came into town for $5,000 … I would be forced to pick the real estate convention. If not for anything else, but for the money.

Weddings give you the freedom to choose.

It puts you in a position of power.

The Greatest Obstacle

Fear.

Very few jobs in photography actually elicit fear.

Weddings top the list.

Let's count the ways:

You could totally have a digital meltdown and all your photographs disappear.

You could actually do a bad job and the bride and family get upset at you.

You could miss a very important shot.

You might be a naturally shy person who isn't used to dealing with groups.

All of these are legit fears.

And you should be scared. Doing weddings is a huge responsibility.

But none of these are insurmountable.

Let's examine them one by one.

The Digital Meltdown Fear

More than legit.

You could actually lose all your data through a computer or a camera malfunction.

If you think it's scary now … imagine the days when we used film.

Here's the first quick fix.

Bring along a photographer friend or pay a photographer to be an assistant.

My assistant photographers get paid on a sliding scale depending on the package. They get anywhere from $70 for a short wedding to $175 for a long wedding.

Set aside $100 of your wedding package to buy an insurance policy—your assistant photographer.

Let your assistant double over everything you shoot.

Make lightning strike twice.

If the wedding is going to be ruined, let it be ruined because your camera accidentally erased all the photos—and so did your assistants.

Can it happen?

Of course.

Is it likely?

Probably not.

Feel free to bring your laptop to the wedding.

At the reception, download and burn all your photos.

If something is STILL messed up, you can always re-shoot something at the reception.

It may be awkward … but at least you have it.

Finally, don't forget to make back-ups over back-ups when you're finished with the wedding.

I require my photographers to have a minimum of 2 copies of their wedding.

One goes to me. And that gets stored in a fire-proof locked cabinet in my studio.

The other copy is kept by the photographer.

And that is the minimum.

Most of my photographers keep two copies for themselves and give one to me.

You Could Do a Bad Job

Yes you could.

And that's why wedding photography is pound for pound, the highest paid profession in photography.

Wedding photographs are among a person's most prized possession.

And people are willing to pay a premium for good photographs.

Start by being confident in your style of photography.

When I first started shooting weddings, I was working for another photographer.

He insisted that I shoot everything on Medium Format.

He has the right to ask that of me—just as I have the right to not take the job.

But as a young photographer, I needed the money. So I learned to shoot a Mamiya 645.

But here was the interesting thing …

After I stopped working for this photographer and branched out on my own—I continued to shoot Medium Format.

And to be honest … I hated it.

Medium format is not for me.

The camera is heavy and there was no automatic focus.

The flash was archaic.

My photos were flat and uninspiring.

I knew I was a good photographer. At the time I worked for the local newspaper as a photographer. And my work there was strong.

My work with my Nikon 35mm camera was dynamic.

I was so proficient with the smaller format and the auto focus.

But back then, it was taboo to shoot a wedding using 35mm.

But I was at a crossroads.

Do I keep shooting Medium Format ... or do I just do what I do best?

I elected to go with the 35mm.

The answer to my fears was just to be comfortable with what I do.

Only you can judge where you are in your career.

But the fact that you're reading this book shows that you're not some amateur.

So be confident in your work and do your thing.

Missing the Shot

Put everything in perspective.

Photographers don't always see things the way the bride sees things.

Brides see things in the macro. Photographers see things in the micro.

In all the years that I've been shooting weddings, I have NEVER had a bride complain that we didn't get the first kiss.

Sometimes we get it ... sometimes we don't.

I have had brides complain that I didn't get a picture of this or that.

One time I had a bride complain that I didn't take enough pictures of her mother-in-law.

Fine. I'll take responsibility for that.

But she also proceeded to tell me that I got tons of pictures of her husband's step mother.

Did you read that right? Yes.

I confused the groom's mother ... for the groom's step mother.

Make sense?

Maybe if you read the above again.

But on the day of the wedding, it's easy to get confused.

Stuff like this happens all the time in weddings.

Sometimes it's your fault. Sometimes it's just a product of circumstance.

But the bottom line is that you are there to do a great job, shoot dynamic pictures and get all the pictures they want.

It that stressful?

Yes.

But is it paralyzing?

No.

Fear of People

Yup.

That is a big one.

One of my photographers is so shy that she looked into taking a public speaking course.

She hasn't yet ... but she's also getting better. So maybe she won't need to.

To be a wedding photographer, you can't be scared of people.

And if you are, you have to be able to fake it.

Wedding photography isn't for everyone.

So if taking control of a group is not for you ... neither is wedding photography.

But it's my suspicion that some of you might be naturally shy people—but want to overcome it.

Truth be told, I am an amazingly shy person.

Only my closest friends know this about me.

Most people that know me publicly or have heard me speak would say otherwise.

But that is because I've developed what is called a persona.

A public persona to be exact.

It's not really being fake.

It's just putting on a suit.

You are not that freshly pressed shirt or those snazzy shoes.

You are a tank top and sweat pants with holes in them.

But you wake up in the morning and spiffy up for the public.

That's what I do as well.

At home … I'm a person who likes holding conversations with my wiener dogs.

But when I leave the house—I become Gene Ho the photographer.

Learn to develop your professional you.

The First Step—Your Portfolio

Ok …

Before you can get into shooting weddings, you need to get a wedding portfolio.

Let's take this in two parts.

I'll go on to talk first about what to do if you're just a start up.

Maybe you have just one or two weddings under your belt.

Maybe you have none.

That's ok. We all had to start somewhere.

So … I'm going to first go over how to get started.

Then after that, I'm going to talk about advanced portfolio ideas after you're already established.

So let's get going.…

Portfolio tips for the Start-up Photographer

The key to any wedding set up is your portfolio.

But it's that old adage … You need experience to get work. But you need work to get experience.

By far, the easiest way to get experience and build a portfolio is working as an assistant to an established photographer.

Sometimes you can make a deal with them. You help out for free or for a low fee. In return, the photographer lets you use the photographs in your portfolio.

However, that is easier said than done.

Most established photographers are very protective on who they have assisting.

So the better way is actually to start building your wedding portfolios based on friend and family weddings.

The easiest way to do this is to approach your friends that are having a wedding, but have already hired another photographer.

Ask them if you can take pictures at their wedding. But promise that you won't get in the way of the other photographer there.

Once you get there, make the most of it.

But whatever you do, don't ask for "alone" time with the bride or groom. Remember, it's still your friend's wedding day—so don't harass them.

Most of all, don't ask to shoot "after" the main photographer.

It's hard enough doing a wedding, let alone setting up a group and having another photographer shoot behind you.

At the best, ask the photographer if you can shoot while he shoots.

There should be no problem if you're respectful.

Whatever you do, just don't ask anyone to "look toward your camera" while you shoot.

Nothing will perturb a photographer more than having a shot where people are looking in different directions.

It will usually take about 3 or 4 weddings to build a portfolio worth to be shown.

Ask your friends or even hire a model to "fill out" your portfolio.

Invite them out, or even pay someone to put on a wedding dress so you can photograph them in popular areas near your city.

Keep in mind that certain places do not allow you to photograph on their property without permission.

If it's a public place, you should have no problem. But for private places and resorts—you need to call ahead.

Some will allow you to shoot there—for a fee.

Don't get offended if they ask that of you.

Most of these resorts spend a lot of money in upkeep and the "privilege" of shooting there is reserved for the guests that hold their wedding at that place.

Two places come to mind for me.

In Charleston, SC, there is a place called Middleton Place.

It's a fine plantation with a rich heritage.

The place is beautiful.

You can do a shoot there, but you have to pay a fee. Not sure, but I think the last time I checked it was more than $100.

To be honest, it's actually worth it.

Another place in Myrtle Beach, SC is the Grande Dunes Beach Club.

This place is stunning.

Because it's a private club, you are not allowed on the property without permission.

Granted the club is more than accommodating if the bride is getting married there.

However, most of the time—it's just a matter of calling up and asking for permission. Sometimes they will grant an exception.

One time I called them up because I was doing the wedding of a former Miss South Carolina.

She wasn't having her wedding there, but wanted a bridal portrait done at the club.

I called up and an exception was made.

Keep in mind, there's a difference between admission price and permission.

In Murrells Inlet, SC, there's a place called Brookgreen Gardens.

You can tour the gardens and see all of the beautiful sculptures for a daily admission price.

But that price does not grant you the right to photograph in there in a professional way.

What you want to do here is build up your wedding portfolio but not step on toes along the way.

Once you get a good collection of wedding photographs—you're ready to go to war.

A common mistake of new photographers is to put together their wedding portfolio based on events.

For example, the photographers say, "Ok … well I need a picture of a cake cutting—so let's use this one. Now I need a picture of a first kiss—so let's use this one."

That is the wrong way of going about it.

I learned this lesson from Joe Gibbs who not only put together winning Super Bowl teams for the Washington Redskins—but has also put together a winning NASCAR team of his own.

One of his secrets is to always go recruit the best possible talent.

Build your team around that talent.

When you're putting together your wedding portfolio—consider your pictures as your players.

Rather than "filing spots"—that is making sure you have one picture of the first kiss, one picture of the cake cutting …

Rather … use the best available pictures you have—regardless of what they are.

From there, put together a nice 30 picture book.

You should have at least one good one of your best photos.

Hopefully, you can get two good albums.

My studio updates our "show books" once a year.

However, when you're first starting out, you should update your portfolio after every wedding.

As far as what kind of albums that you will use to show off your photo—that is simple.

Use whatever album you're going to plan on giving the bride.

I'll address different styles of books in a later chapter.

But for now, know that the most important thing is to get a good collection of photographs.

Portfolio Tips for Advanced Photographers

Alright. Maybe by the time you read (or reread) this chapter—you have a good amount of weddings under your belt.

That's a good thing.

From here, let's consider some ways to improve your portfolio:

Go for Emotion: **When you're deciding which pictures to keep and which pictures to toss—keep in mind that there is one best seller. Emotion.**

Make sure that each picture in your portfolio demonstrates emotion.

How you define that is a little difficult.

But look at the picture.

Does it make you laugh? Cry?

Does it make you feel happy?

Could you imagine yourself in that picture?

That is generally why I avoid putting too many formal pictures in my portfolio.

A picture of the bride with her mother staring straight in camera might mean a lot to the bride. But it means little to me and you. It means little to the newly engaged lady looking at your portfolio.

But take that same picture where the bride is kissing her mother on the cheek.

Her mom is laughing uncontrollably. Now that is different.

That shows raw emotion. That sells.

Make your Pictures Complimentary: Wedding portfolios are a little different than say a model portfolio or a family portrait portfolio.

Generally, all the other sample books are what we call "stand-alone" pictures.

For example, if you're showing off your modeling work … each turn of the page has one picture on the right hand side. And the left hand side is blank.

This is not a rule … just a generality.

But it's done that way, so that each picture should allow for the greatest impact without a distraction from a picture on the left hand side.

However, wedding portfolios are different.

Because most of the time—there is a picture on the left hand side—and the right hand side.

That's mainly because it is how the bride will get their final product—their wedding album.

Knowing this—make sure that your show book has complimentary photos in it.

If there's a groom on the left hand side … put a bride on the right hand side.

If there's a picture of the wedding cake on the left hand side, a great picture of the bride and groom cutting the cake would be perfect on the right hand side.

This is what you call complimentary photos.

Now the challenge in putting together a good show book is having your pictures strong enough that you can basically go in any direction you want to.

For example, you might have a fantastic picture of a wedding cake that might be perfect. But you don't have any fantastic pictures of a couple cutting a cake.

The more weddings you do, the more you will find good pieces to fit. Dynamic pictures that fit.

So if you do have a good appropriate photo that fits—all the better.

If not, the challenge is to find one that does—or scrap the great picture of the cake.

A lot of times, I will end up with mismatched photos. They are great photos. It's just that I don't have any complimentary photo to go with it.

When you are finding photos that complement each other—also consider the tonal range of the picture.

The easiest way to find pictures with the same tonal range of the picture is by having the left side picture come from the same wedding as the picture on the right side.

Chances are the lighting will be about the same. The color balance will be similar.

The pictures will compliment each other.

On the other hand, it would be very unlikely that I would ever put a sunset picture on the left hand side and a daylight beach picture on the right hand side.

They don't compliment each other.

The Complete Wedding Book: **If you're a new photographer to the wedding scene—you're going to get smoked if someone asks you to see a complete wedding.**

Not that you're a bad photographer.

It's just that not everything you're going to do is going to be great and wonderful with three or four weddings under your belt.

But there comes a time in every wedding photographer's career where someone will ask them to see a complete wedding.

A seasoned photographer should have one ready.

This is probably one of the harder portfolios to put together.

Remember, the album your brides put together is not necessarily the same album that will attract other brides to you.

Their album means something to THEM. You have to put together an album that will appeal to someone else.

To do this is not easy.

But again, you're looking for emotion.

One trick that I use during weddings is what I call the candid formal.

I know that sounds funny. It's a contradiction.

But this is how it's done.

Right after I finish the boring, but very necessary formal picture of the bride and groom with their parents, then I tell them, "That's it ... we got it. You're done."

Then you make a show of putting down the camera.

The natural reaction to someone finishing their formal pictures is one of relief and excitement.

They usually look at each other and smile or laugh.

At this point, immediately put your camera back up and take a picture.

You just got a "candid formal."

Try filling up your portfolio with shots like these.

Whatever you do ... avoid the photos of the group shots where the people are looking dead into the camera.

That means the world to the bride in it. It means nothing to everyone else.

Avoid the Deal Breaker: **I've seen it so many times.**

You're looking through a portfolio and everything is so nice. Everything is flowing. It's all good.

Then with the next turn of the page, you see something that just makes you say, "What in the world?"

Two pictures come to mind.

One was a photographer that had a picture of a bride posing with a can of Coke.

Don't ask.

I can only assume that the bride worked for Coca-cola or something.

But there she was.

The bride is standing there with a Coke and a smile.

The second picture that comes to mind was a little more understandable—but just over the top.

It was a picture of a bride with an umbrella and she is walking through a graveyard.

I'm sure you can guess.

The bride probably lost her mother, father or a very dear family member. And on her wedding day—she visits the grave.

Yes. If you're doing the wedding and the bride wants that picture—then take it.

But to put that picture in your wedding show book is just plain creepy. Sorry. Just my opinion.

Here's why those photographers chose that picture. And here's the lesson for us.

Those pictures that we talked about—the bride probably loved it.

It was probably the bride's favorite picture in her album.

She probably went on and on about it.

But here's the thing …

Just because a bride loves that picture, doesn't mean everyone else is going to "get it."

It's kind of like pictures of your pet.

I have a picture of my weiner dog where she's just looking at the camera in such a goofy way.

The picture is actually blurry.

But I love it.

Because when I look at that picture, it means the world to me.

It's the look my puppy gives me when she knows she did something wrong.

But to be honest, it's a bad picture. And it also means NOTHING to anyone else but me.

When you put together your show books … make sure the picture is self explanatory.

One of my photographers, Kevin Teachey, coined a good phrase.

He is one of the instructors at the college where I teach.

He said this, "If you have to explain why the picture is good, then it's not good."

Court Controversy: **Give your portfolio a little edge.**

Two pictures come to mind in my show books over the years. One was taken from Kevin.

It was a picture of the groom walking down the beach with his friends.

What was interesting about it was that he was smoking a cigarette with sunglasses on.

To be honest, it was a pretty tough-looking photo. It almost looked like something from a movie poster.

The picture was just enough to be on the edge. But it wasn't enough to be the deal killer.

This picture got people thinking. It made people stop and look. It was so unusual.

Half the people stopped and commented how the groom looked like a jerk.

The other half commented how that picture reminded them exactly of what their future husband was like.

Call that any way you want. But it stopped and got people thinking.

Another photo that came to mind was a wedding that I took where the bride wore a bright red wedding dress.

I never have seen anything quite like it before.

The dress was bright red.

It was more than unique.

But the bride did have sense of humor about it.

On her wedding cake, instead of the traditional bride and groom "cake topper," she had one specially made.

The "cake topper" groom was in traditional black. And the "cake topper" bride was painted red.

The response was very much like the groom smoking the cigarette.

Except half of the people thought the bride in the red dress was certifiably crazy.

The other half thought she was the coolest person in the world.

The game here is to move your viewers.

You want to use your portfolio to draw people into conversations.

But be careful. Don't go over the top.

The conversation should be based on the personalities or the choices of the bride and groom.

It should not be based upon your choice as a photographer to include the photo in your show book.

However, even in the case where you have several controversial photos, use them sparingly.

The bulk of your portfolio should still be based on the raw emotion of fun and love.

Finding the Brides

Take this chapter with a grain of salt.

Do a good job on your wedding and the brides will find you.

Think of each bride you shoot as your personal marketing agent.

You do a great job, you make the bride look beautiful—and she will show that book to everyone she meets.

So your primary job is to do such a fantastic job that the bride can't help but to brag about your work.

But you still have to be public. You still have to find a way get people to look at you show books.

So here I will discuss several of the main ways to reach your brides.

Website: This is your absolute minimum.

When I first started in wedding photography … having a website was a luxury item.

I was the first photographer in my area to have a website.

It was very archaic.

Pretty much it was a "forward slash" website.

By that I mean I piggy-backed off of a friend's domain.

It wasn't a website as much as it was a web page.

I can't remember the domain name, but it ended with "/genehophotography"

The closest analogy I can think about is my "myspace" page which is www. myspace.com/genehophotography.

That's fine for a myspace page. But today it would be very insufficient.

But back then, it was way more than what any other photographer had.

Today, you should have at the very minimum a website with a dedicated domain name.

I picked, www.geneho.com.

I also own www.genehophotography.com … but I leave it blank.

I just bought that domain name so no one else could own it.

I vigorously advertise and push the geneho.com site.

If I had to give up everything and all forms of advertising except one—I would keep my website and domain name.

If you haven't already, make sure you acquire your appropriate domain name.

It could be your name. It could be the name of your company.

Of course, now it is easier said than done.

If your studio name is remotely generic, it has probably already been bought up by another photographer.

Or, if you're using your name—it could have been bought up someone else with the same name (though they probably aren't in the photography business).

From there, your choices are limited.

You could attempt to contact the owner of the domain name and negotiate to buy that name.

However, the other option is to go with a .net, address.

Personally, I would never own a .net.

That's because most people think first of .com.

And the danger is to have someone log another website thinking that the photos they see are yours.

I would personally much rather get a good .com domain name that is cleverly worded.

It might be a "twist" on your studio name.

But either way, think carefully. Find something that works. Promote it and protect it.

I have a five-year contract or "dibs" on my name, www.geneho.com.

But you can be sure that I will renew my contract way before then.

That being said, the more important thing is what you will put on your site.

Most of the photographers that read this already have their website or domain name reserved or picked out.

So let's get to the meat of this.

The first thing to figure out is your strategy.

You must decide the feel of your website.

Ten years ago, I had five photographers working for my studio.

While that's a fairly good number for a privately owned studio—I still wanted to project my studio as bigger than what it was.

So I took the strategy to have the "feel" of my website as being very corporate.

I would refer to photographers and my studio in a very cold "corporate" style.

I would use the following phrases:

"If you would like to contact one of our photographers ..."

"For more information, please call us at ..."

"Your photographer will arrive at your wedding ..."

Basically, I was trying to convey the idea that Gene Ho Photography was NOT "mom and pop."

We were a big corporation that could be trusted to do your wedding.

And to be honest, that worked very well for my studio as we were growing.

In time, a lot of photographers adopted this feel.

Now it's very common for photographers to give a mystic of being bigger than they really are.

And that's not necessarily a bad thing.

Sometimes that can be very effective.

Maybe you're working out of your home. Maybe you don't have a physical studio location.

In that case, a strategy like this might work.

However, it can be overdone.

I visited one photographer's website who I knew for a certainty was a "one-man" studio.

But the photographer had on his website, "For more information, please contact our customer service department …"

Wow … that's interesting.

I have a lot of photographers now, but I still don't have a customer service department unless you count Nadean sitting next to me.

So if you go that route and that feel, be careful that you don't overdo it.

Today, my studio is very big.

Most people that deal with me know that I'm very well established.

So recently I decided to take a different strategy for my website.

If you go to my website now, it has a very "down home" feel to it.

Instead of saying …

"For more information, please call us at …"

Now my website says something to the effect of, "Hey … if you like what you see here, send me an email …"

Instead of saying …

"Your photographer will arrive at your wedding …"

Now I say something like, "When I get to your wedding, the first thing that I like to do is …"

The point is I try to make myself as real as possible.

Now everybody is doing a, "… call our customer service department" route.

So I decided to do the switch-a-roo and go with the "mom and pop" style.

And to be honest, I like it that way.

The only thing I don't know is what my website will look and feel like five years from now.

Who knows.

Maybe I'll go back to the corporate feel.

I don't know.

But I do know that I will pick a decidedly definitive feel for the website and let it roll from there.

As far as what pictures to put on your website—the same rule applies as what we talked about with the show books.

Go for emotion.

Move your viewers.

I have to just relate a story to you.

I know it might sound really self serving. But it's a true story and it's something you can learn from.

Nadean was working a bridal show with Andy.

One bride came up to our booth and started crying.

She mentioned that the photos moved her that much.

Wow.

That means so much to me.

But at the same time, it's what I strive to do with my photos.

I try to make people cry.

I try to make people laugh.

So … from time to time, it shouldn't surprise me if that happens.

It's what we strive to do.

Bridal Shows: In all its glory, bridal shows are either the biggest blessing or biggest curse.

The nationwide average for a bridal show booth is now about $700.

It depends on what city you go to.

I've been to shows costing as much as $1,500.

I've also been to shows costing as little as $275.

And I've been to a few "free" shows.

In a nutshell, bridal shows are where you pay for the right to display your goods and services in front of future brides.

Oddly enough, most of these brides also pay an admission price to have the right to view your goods and services.

Just search the Internet and you'll find tons of them in all kinds of cities.

Of course, you will probably first try to find one near the city where you live.

However, this can get a little difficult.

Most bridal show companies limit the booths that they sell to photographers.

After all, they don't want to put on a show with only photographers.

Ideally most shows want an equal spread of photographers, florists, caterers, reception venues, etc.

Knowing this, it can be a challenge trying to even get into a show.

However, the laws of attrition will work in your favor.

Let's go back to what I said about bridal shows being either a blessing or a curse.

At first glance, it would seem like a no-brainer for a photographer to do a bridal show.

After all, we're actually in the best position to capitalize on it.

Even if the bridal show costs $800, you can technically make that back on the first booking you get.

But here's the thing.

It's easier said than done.

In more than 10 years of doing bridal shows, I've seen a ton of photographers come and go.

Why is that?

It's because they go to these bridal shows and they get smoked.

They pay their $800 or so … and they get several interviews. But they don't book any weddings.

How is it possible to get "shut out" at a bridal show?

It's very simple.

If the show features 10 photographers, then you have 10 photographers coming in with guns blazing.

Everybody is putting their best foot forward.

And when that happens, there's a definitive line between who the good photographers are and who are just getting by.

If I can use the analogy, it's like going to a bodybuilding competition.

You see someone walking down the street with an incredible build.

And you say, "Wow ... that guy has the perfect body."

But then you put him in a room with 25 guys that work out just as much, and suddenly you can see the flaws.

Probably the first five years that I worked as a photographer, I didn't do a single bridal show.

To be honest, it wasn't necessary.

At the time, my smallest package was $450.

Today, that seems so little.

But when I was making $410 a week as photojournalist, $450 for a few hours on a Saturday was a big deal.

So I didn't need to work bridal shows, because even if I got three weddings from it—it would barely pay my booth rental.

Now that's not to say new photographers need to stay away from bridal shows.

Actually, other than your website—I think it's the most effective form of advertisement.

But proceed with caution. And go there ready to play with the big boys.

So say you're already doing bridal shows or you're ready to get into the arena.

Then good for you.

In a nutshell, you will need several show books. I'd say a minimum of three.

You will need your rate cards or some sort of hand out.

And you will need some sort of big display in the background.

If you're already doing bridal shows, I know you know this.

But let's discuss this and see where you can improve.

First, the show books:

This is basically the same show book that we talked about earlier. It is your portfolio.

Very similar to your website, the key is to have a strategy.

Some photographers like to go with what I call the Zerg strategy.

Zerg is a term coined by online gamers. It basically means that you're throwing everything but the kitchen sink out there in hopes that something sticks.

By far, this is the most common strategy.

Basically, the photographer puts as much crap out as they are able to on the table.

They have their parent albums, they have their show books. They have big photos. They have small photos.

I've even seen such ridiculous things as key chains with pictures on it.

The photographer is trying to show off all their products in their little 10'x10' booth.

I see this all the time and I think it's the worst strategy.

Each bride, at best, is spending 5 minutes looking at your work.

If you overwhelm them with "stuff," you're not going to leave them with any great impression.

Now I don't do it, but have seen some other strategies that people use that I think is pretty nifty.

I've seen some go with a hi-tech approach.

Some put together a slide show on a flat screen television.

Others have these super custom built booths.

I have to applaud them.

Some of them look fantastic.

Personally, I think the most important thing is to have some sort of strategy.

And if funky lighting and hi-tech slide shows are your thing—then that is great.

I change out my strategy from time to time.

But for the most part, I usually go for a minimalist approach.

I kind of like my work and the work of my photographers to stand on itself.

But that's not to say that in the future I won't take another strategy.

Last winter I tried to do something different.

If you've seen my website, you'll know that I'm involved with stock car racing.

The Gene Ho Photography Chevy is a beast.

In the past, Jason Jarrett drove the car.

Jason Jarrett is the son of NASCAR legend Dale Jarrett.

During one bridal show in Myrtle Beach, I was trying to arrange the race car and Jason Jarrett to be in my booth.

It would have been great.

The guys that got dragged into the show would have a great time checking out the car and meeting Jason.

On the other hand, their future bride could have a great time looking at our show books.

It never worked out.

Basically, most bridal shows are held on Sunday and most teams and drivers are racing on the weekend.

But it was a cool thought. And I still might do that one day.

Another way you can improve if you're already doing bridal shows is to improve your handouts:

In the later chapters, I'll talk about rate cards.

I have always been very open about my wedding rates.

I don't know how the idea came about, but when I first started weddings, all the photographers would hide the fact that they even had a rate card.

And they would never distribute it at the bridal shows.

I never understood why they did that.

I've been told that they want people to actually come to their studio first and fall in love with their photographs.

That somehow people would go to their studio and love their show book so much that it wouldn't matter how much it cost to book them.

Hey ... if that's the case, then go for it.

But I know that when I go to shop for a car, I pretty much want to know what it will cost.

And I know that most of my brides appreciate that I'm open about my pricing.

For me, it's pretty simple. I publish my prices and tell them what they get for each package.

And I openly distribute this at the bridal shows.

Note. I openly distribute it.

From time to time, I get rival photographers that think they have to trick me into giving them my rate card.

I can't tell you how funny that is.

Sometimes I can pick out the "friend of a rival photographer" that comes up to our booth and poses as a bride.

It's so funny when that happens. It's so transparent.

But it's all good.

They actually don't even need to waste their time.

They can find my rates on my website.

And now, if they want to find out how I do things, they could just buy my book.

I'm very open about this because when it all boils down to it, it's all about the photography.

So my advice is pretty simple when it comes to your bridal show handouts.

I like giving out my rate card which is also my basic promotional piece.

You can choose to give it out or not.

But at least you need something to help them remember you at the end of the day.

By the way, it's funny to see how smart these brides are.

I've seen everything.

Some brides will put your rate card in a different bag.

As you could imagine, one bag is the "throw out" bag. The other bag is the "keep" bag.

Another interesting thing I've seen brides do is take our rate card and "dog ear" the corner.

Evidently (and I hope!) that means they are going to call all the business cards and or brochures that have a bent corner on them.

At the end of the day, the most important thing is for you to make some sort of impression on the bride.

That's why it's so important to have a great and dynamic website.

I know what goes on.

These brides take all their brochures home.

They throw them on the bed and sort them all out.

Your hope is that they keep your hand-out and either go on your website or give you a call.

So that's why the next point is so important …

Your big display:

Besides your rate card and our hand-out brochure …

Besides your show books …

You will need some sort of background display.

The simplest by far is to get two or three framed 16x20 pictures and put them up on an easel.

I've done this plenty of times before.

Another option is to buy some sort of stand-alone backdrop and hang some pictures on it.

I've done that too.

I've also seen everything else in the book.

And some of them are pretty cool and innovative.

Again … I like to go as plain as possible.

Maybe plain isn't a good word.

Probably a better word is: simple.

I like to have two or three marquee pictures.

My strategy here is to have it be something they can remember.

For example, in the past, I've matched my background display to my rate card.

This way people could make the connection later on.

When they see my rate card, it's my hope that they remember me.

So I use my background display photos as a tool to do that.

It should be fun.

You're basically there to show your face and to give people a first impression.

The way I think of it, is that you're not so much striving for a "yes."

You're really striving to not get a, "no."

The brides will size you and your studio up.

And if you can get away without getting an "absolutely not," then you're doing well.

Ultimately, it's going to be about your photos and their comfort level with you.

So relax and have fun.

Traditional Advertisements: **When it comes to me, I think I've done it all.**

You name it.

Granted I've also done more than my fair share of non-traditional advertising.

I would hardly call sponsoring a race car as traditional.

But here is a brief list of some of the ads I've done.

Newspaper.

Magazine.

Billboards.

Those little direct mailer envelopes where people give out coupons for free oil changes. (Oye … was that a mistake.)

Yellow Pages.

Internet Banners.

Movie Theatre Billboards.

Radio.

Let's see … did I leave anything out?

If you can think of something, let me know. I probably did that too.

Through all the good, bad and ugly—I've come up with an advertising strategy.

Advertising doesn't work for photographers. Marketing does.

Let me explain the difference.

While for the most part, the words can be interchangeable, I'm going to give my take at it.

Advertising is where you put out an ad and people react to it by doing something.

In general, your neighborhood car dealer advertises.

You hear their ads all the time on the radio.

"Come in this weekend and get $500 cash back off any car."

Or, you might hear, "This weekend only, get a minimum $6,000 trade in."

The car dealership is trying to advertise for you to go in and spend money with them.

On the other hand, the car manufacturer in Detroit generally works on marketing.

They are the ones that put out the fancy ads in glossy magazines.

"The Strongest Truck in its Class."

"Pure luxury … it's affordable."

Whatever.

Basically, they are marketing.

You're not going to buy a truck … but if you know someone who is, you're going to want to get their truck—because it's the most powerful one.

You might not be ready to buy a luxury car, but when you do—you'll buy theirs because their car is luxurious and affordable.

When it comes to wedding photography, marketing works best.

I have seen advertising when it comes to other aspects of photography.

Every year, my friend would run a small ad in the area newspaper during Valentine's Day.

"Get your pictures done this weekend and get 2 free 8x10's."

And that works well.

But could you imagine an ad saying …

"Get engaged by this Friday and get $300 off any of our wedding packages."

It doesn't work that way.

So concentrate on marketing.

And have a strategy.

I've used several over the years.

When I was working to open and solidify a new market in Wilmington, NC, I came up with this strategy:

It was a simple ad in a wedding magazine with several beautiful pictures.

But the only text was my logo (that also included my website) and the words, "Upscale Wilmington's Premier Wedding Photographer."

That's it.

It didn't even have my studio's phone number on it.

It was a definitive statement strategy.

We're the best and we serve the upscale.

And we're so sure of ourselves that we don't even need to list our phone number.

The plan worked. And since then with hard work and great photography—we are the premier wedding photographer in that city.

Granted much to the ire of the local photographers there.

But no one ever said this is supposed to be fair,

Fortunately or unfortunately, we're not always going to be able to get along.

More on that later with my subheading on "Alliances."

Another marketing strategy that I've seen effectively done (but I have not yet tried), is the "I'm the relaxed wedding photographer," line.

Basically, the photographer shows off one of their funny pictures and has the tagline, "Fun and Relaxed."

What the photographer is trying to convey is, "Hey, the other wedding photographers are stiff and boring … But I'm fun. So pick me!"

I like that.

I think that's a good plan.

Think carefully of how you want to craft your reputation and market that effectively.

Word of Mouth: You can't ignore this one.

There are two primary ways to generate word of mouth.

One is the tried and true form of word of mouth.

That is when you actually get your clients, your brides, to brag on you.

That goes back to doing a great job and taking excellent pictures.

A friend of mine takes this one step further.

He actually keeps a mailing list of all his clients.

Each month, he puts together a newsletter were he lists the weddings that he's booked with a "congratulations on your engagement" guise.

Basically, what he wants people to see is the name of someone they know.

Then those brides go to their friend whom they also see listed—and they go, "Hey, girlfriend. Cool. You're like me. You could only afford that cheap-ass photographer."

No … just kidding.

They look on the list, see someone they know and that fosters conversation the next time those two meet.

It's really a great idea.

I haven't done it yet. But that's because I haven't gone with that strategy.

But I don't blame my friend for producing that newsletter.

Right now, the way I like to generate word of mouth is by reaching the vendors they will use.

I'm talking about the florist, the church, the caterer.

The idea behind what I do here is to take care of everyone associated with the wedding.

I do that by finding out who the vendors are at each wedding I do.

Then after I finish the wedding and the bride has her photos (I make sure that the bride gets her pictures first.)—I then pick out some photos for the vendor.

We try to do it at every wedding we photograph.

The florist, caterer or whomever can always use some free photos of the wedding they just did.

And after a while, your reputation will grow.

And the next time that bride runs into that vendor, chances are they will talk about you and the great job you did.

One notable wedding that came to mind.

In Atlanta, my studio is frequently hired by the Atlanta Falcons to photograph their cheerleaders.

Tear.

I know that's a rough job.

After doing this for several years, I really do get to know the girls really well.

And since then, I've done more than a handful of the cheerleader's weddings.

In Atlanta, one of the most exclusive and beautiful places to get married is Chateau Elan.

Wow … that place is fascinating.

It's built on the side of a massive winery.

Recently, one of the Falcon Cheerleaders got married there.

As you could imagine, it was just a beautiful wedding.

Pretty people. Pretty place.

In Atlanta, the Falcon Cheerleaders are celebrities.

After all, they are professional cheerleaders.

It's kind of like in high school where the captain of the cheerleaders wears a new outfit and suddenly it's a cool style.

Who knows what the psychology of that is?

But it works later on in life too.

If you've ever met a professional cheerleader, you'll find that they are extremely talented and professional.

Most have great jobs outside of cheerleading.

I know one of the Falcon Cheerleaders is the assistant to the First Lady of Georgia … the Governor's wife.

Another Cheerleader performed on American Idol.

They have a great reputation.

Knowing this, after the wedding I sent Chateau Elan a complimentary wedding album of the event.

And I made sure the text was put on it … "Atlanta Falcon's Cheerleader Shannon. Her wedding at Chateau Elan by Gene Ho."

That album earned me the referral of the venue. Not to mention, endless word of mouth for future brides.

Alliances: Alright. Get ready for the juicy stuff. The dirt.

Here we go …

Among photographers in the areas near my studios—I am hated.

Here is why.

The way things used to run was this:

A photographer would work as a start-up.

At first he does a year or two of low-dollar weddings just to get his name out.

Eventually, he gets a name out there.

He raises his price to market levels and in time he's booked out for the weekends in the year.

Finally, when I reached this level, I was supposed to do what everyone else did.

I was "supposed" to raise my prices.

I was supposed to raise it to the point where I would earn the same amount, but would only work only 1/3 the amount.

After all, that is how I got a foothold in my first studio.

The big-dog in the area at the time was Leon Adelstone. He was so successful that he raised his prices so high that few people could afford him.

He went from working maybe 30 weddings a year to about 15 to 10 to 5. Just a guess.

And as he worked less … he made just as much.

It also allowed someone like me to get a foothold on the area. That's because I was working the mid-priced weddings.

But when Leon retired to Florida, here is what I did.

I didn't raise my prices.

I kept it the same.

And that's ok. But even then, if I'm booked 50 weekends a year—shouldn't I start making recommendations to other photographers?

Normally that would be the status quo.

But now I have 20 other trained photographers.

When I'm booked, I will book my trusted photographers next.

Basically, I never kicked the door open for the other studios.

And that has caused a source of contention. We were supposed to share.

Some days in Myrtle Beach, SC, we are doing every wedding going on that day.

We are dominating.

There are some days where we're doing the first afternoon wedding at a venue. And then when that wedding finishes, we're also doing the evening wedding at that same place.

To put it mildly, we're putting an ass-stomping in this area.

I bring this up, because it's rare to have a studio like mine in any given market.

I know they exist, but they are rare.

To manage a studio the way I do it, is very difficult.

You basically have to find good talent and find a way to keep them.

But this is the way that I chose to run my studio. And it is unorthodox.

But at the same time, it boils down to strategy.

This is the business model I chose.

In this case, my strategy is to find great photographers. I find dynamic photographers with great personalities.

Then I bring them into my business as profit-sharing partners.

It's not a new concept.

It's very similar to a law firm.

A law firm is very interesting because in the United States, people have the right to choose their own lawyer.

So if you're working at a law firm, nothing stops you with walking off with your employer's clients.

As a lawyer, you have that right.

So, what most law firms do is bring their successful attorneys in as partners.

After all, if you end up with 100 clients, your employer isn't going to want you to leave with them and start your own firm.

So after a while, your employer is going to cut you a deal and make you a partner.

There are some firms with literally hundreds of partners in it.

And most of them are happy to work in a law firm that doesn't have their name on the building.

After all, they get more work working as a whole than they would by themselves.

Part of it is their hustle in getting clients … part of it is the reputation of the firm as a whole.

That is how I chose to structure my studio.

And it has worked in a big way.

You would probably have to go five or six photographers deep on my staff to find someone who is working fewer weddings per year, and making less money per year than my closest competitor.

But I know this is not how it's usually done.

Whether you're a start-up or an existing working wedding photographer—your next key to survival is having good alliances.

But no photographer is going to be in an alliance with me. I know that.

That is because I will never return a favor and refer another studio.

Why should I if I have enough photographers to field almost every demand?

And that's ok.

But if you're on your own, choose your alliances carefully.

Basically, find another photographer in your area who you like and whose work you respect.

And all you're doing is asking them to throw a referral to you when they are already booked.

In return, you will do the same.

It's actually better to keep your circle of referral photographers small.

There is just no way to be all things to all people.

I know one unscrupulous business man. Not a photographer, by the way, but he is in the wedding industry.

This man is what we call a turd.

He tries to be all things to all people.

His referral list is as big as this book.

But does he return the favor?

Hardly.

He can't. He has too many people he claims he's "in with."

And most of them are rivals.

You can't do this. And it catches up to you.

You can't be all things to all people.

Sooner or later you're going to be called up to the plate be asked to pick a side.

It's kind of like international politics.

You can claim to be someone's ally and yet also claim to be neutral.

Governments for the most part do all they can to avoid war.

And in our generation, a lot of time that comes down to a trade embargo. It's a way to get a country to see things their way.

I'm not advocating it, it's just what happens.

That's why when a country is unruly and not doing things that are just ... then countries put sanctions on other countries.

It's just the way it is.

My good friend owns a limousine company. He's a straight up guy.

And I'm also friends with other limousine company owners.

And trust me; I try to stay out of the fray as much as possible.

I know the limousine scene has dirty laundry and bones to pick with each other.

But when my friend told me how one company did something dishonest with his company ... I'm going to stand behind my friend.

Today, I won't recommend this other limousine company that did my friend wrong.

Granted, I'm not going to go out of my way to harm that business.

But I'm sure going to set the record straight if someone asks me my opinion about them or if they want me as a reference.

It's not how I like it.

Actually, I'd rather play nice.

But when someone does my ally wrong; I'm going to stick beside them.

After all, they've been good to me.

Here's an interesting thing that happened to me—and I more than respect it.

Last year, we had one day that was completely sold out.

All my photographers were working.

We've done this before. But usually when we do and prospective brides call in, we just tell them we're sold out.

That's all good and well.

But this one time, we had this bride that I knew personally. We did her sister's wedding.

It drove me crazy to just send her away.

I'll be honest; I really wanted to see if I could do it.

I thought maybe I could call up a photographer that used to work for me and ask her for one more favor.

But after much discussion, the consensus with the studio photographers was a no go.

I make a lot of my decisions based on how my photographers view things.

But in this case, no one trusted this former photographer anymore.

And it wasn't just MY reputation that would have taken a hit if something went wrong. It would have been the whole studio collectively.

So I was basically vetoed by my own staff.

And I'm cool with that.

So we decided that there was one photographer in Myrtle Beach that I really liked.

He never worked for me.

So he had his own style and way of doing things.

It was different, but good.

So I had Nadean call him up and give him the name of the bride and the information.

And he was available.

But on the phone, before he hung up, he told Nadean this …

"You realize that I could never return the favor to you? You realize that if any one of the other photographers knew I gave you a wedding referral that I would be in trouble."

What a beautiful line.

Here is a stand-up guy.

Nadean laughed and basically told him that she knew that, but we really wanted this young bride to have good pictures.

Personally, I love it. Even though I will never get that favored returned—it's nice to see people being straight up and loyal to his friends.

His friends—oddly enough, are my rivals.

But good for him.

That photographer is a success now, and will continue to be a success.

Being loyal to your friends is a good thing.

Even if they are my rivals.

Rate Cards and your Stable of Products

When it comes to your rate cards and your stable of products, a lot depends upon what is easiest and practical for you.

Let's talk about your rate cards first.

When I first started in wedding photography, it was hard to find a rate card for any photographer.

Photographers would keep it a secret.

I guess they didn't want other photographers to figure out what they were doing. I guess they were afraid someone would undercut them? I don't know.

But today it's well established that you have to have some sort of rate card.

You need to have some sort of "menu" of goods and services.

I do know that in the late 90s it was in vogue in California not to have wedding packages at all.

The way it was generally done is that photographers would charge a flat "sitting fee" for the wedding.

Most of the time it would be something real reasonable, like $500 or so.

But with that, the bride got "zip."

After the wedding, they would still need to go back to the photographer's studio and then they would purchase the pictures they wanted.

I don't know for sure, but I figured that when it was all said and done, they would get about the same as what I charge now for weddings.

Not that that's a bad idea. I'm sure that system worked for them.

Interestingly enough, that's still how I work my general portraits at my studio.

People come to me, they pay a sitting fee. And with that, they get nothing.

Then they have to visit my studio again and then order pictures.

That works well for portraits, but I never liked that idea for a wedding.

The reason being is that I know that I have a budget. And I like to know exactly what I'm spending and what I'm going to be getting.

So today I use the package method.

I basically sat down one night and did the entire math.

I figured out what it would cost for me to get them the product. I figured out what it would cost to get the albums. And I figured out what I wanted at the end.

And I came up with four packages.

And there is no secret to it.

It's posted right on my website.

And it's simple.

For every package you get three things …

You get the time of the photographer.

You get your proofs (which are real 4x5 frame-able photos).

And you get your album.

And basically the higher up you go in the package realm, the more time or the more "products" you get.

I took all of this information and I put it in two places.

I put it on my website. And I also put it in a printable version which I call my rate card.

My rate card is a nifty little brochure.

It changes once a year, but the main components stay the same.

There are a few pictures on it.

There's the actual rates listed.

There are some words on it that give a basic rundown of what we do.

I mass produce this every November and a give these out at bridal shows and to prospective brides.

But how you choose to put together your rate card is up to you.

Over the years, I've actually made them out of card stock. Sometimes they were made out of glossy brochure paper.

I have seen other photographer make their "rate card" out of a folder and put unbound stationary paper with information on it.

It really doesn't matter what you do, but make sure it's nice. Make sure it's cost effective.

In a way, your rate card might be even more difficult to produce that your website.

On your website, you can put as little or as much information as you want.

On a rate card, you want to be able to say much as you can in the smallest amount of space possible.

In the past, my rate cards have been as big as a six-panel foldout. It has also been as small as a two-sided 6x9 card.

Be selective in the pictures you put on it and the information you give out.

To save space on my current rate card, I put the wedding packages down—but I omitted my "a la carte" prices.

To save space, I didn't go through the different reprint prices and the various upgrades costs to things such as canvas finishes.

Maybe later on I'll create a rate card with this information on it. But for now, I just use a separate print-out for those miscellaneous items.

How you chose to do it is of course up to you.

But I strongly suggest a clean, easy to understand rate card.

I've seen some rate cards in the past that look like something from an accountant's desk.

The photographer listed his prices. Then he listed his alternate prices if you wanted all your pictures to have an upgraded finish.

Then he had another alternate of the alternate prices if you wanted all your pictures to come back with an extra U.V. coating on it.

I kid you not.

Then I have seen other photographers include a list of different "touch-up" options.

For me, I don't even want you to see a picture that I took without me fixing it up in Photoshop.

I couldn't even imagine me trying to sell you a picture like that and trying to make you pay more for the touch-ups.

The way I feel about touch-ups is that it's part of your job as a photographer.

Everything that leaves my studio is a finished picture. It's edited, cropped and touched up.

Some photographers don't feel that way, and that's their decision.

But I always find it funny when I run into a rate card that has a menu of touch-ups …

Remove Wrinkles—$10 per face.

Remove Stray Hairs—$15 per picture.

Breast Lift—$18 per breast.

Just kidding on the last one.

"Ummm … can we save money and you just lift the one breast?"

You're here to shoot great photos and having great Photoshop skills is just part of our job as a modern-day photographer. Period.

As far as your other stable of products—keep these simple as well.

Sure. You could always make exceptions. You could always customize a package for someone.

But make things easy on your clients.

Currently, we get all our albums from two companies.

The one company handles our more traditional albums.

These are the ones that you see all the time.

They are the leather-covered album. You open them up and there is the picture there held in place by a cut mat.

Our studio offers only two versions of this.

One is a 5x7 30-print album. The other is an 8x10 30-print album.

If someone wants to have a larger album or add pages … we can be very accommodating.

But we sampled a lot of books until we found the one that was right for our studio.

Do the same.

Also … most album distributors allow you to purchase one or two albums a year at a discount. Use these for your studio samples.

The other company we use makes our flush-mounted "magazine" albums.

These are the more modern looking albums where the pages ARE the photos.

The best way to describe it is that it looks like a well made, high-quality coffee-table book.

We call these albums the Fusion Album.

As far as the other products we offer … they include everything from framed 16x20 Canvas pictures to Wallet Sized Thank You Cards.

Actually selecting and building your stable of products is one of the more enjoyable parts of being a wedding photographer.

You get to scour the Internet and check out all the new products.

You get to request samples and debate amongst your friends the validity and the desirability of each product.

Not all products are actual "items."

Some are just normal pictures repackaged a different way.

Our Wallet Sized Thank You Cards are nothing more than 100 wallets.

But we slap a "Thank You! Joe and Betty" on it—and suddenly it's a product.

But it's popular and a great seller.

Another new product we've been offering is the "Hi-Res CD of Your Wedding."

Yup … You guessed it guys.

For a price, we're also giving them the "negatives" to the wedding.

We're giving them a Hi-Res disk with their pictures on it so they can take their pictures anywhere and reprint them at the least possible prices.

In essence, we're killing all hopes for our studio of ever making any more money on reprints.

But it's a choice I'm going to go with and gamble with in today's economy.

Back in the day of using film, this was not only unthinkable, but almost taboo in the photographic community.

But it is what it is.

On an interesting side note ...

The reports I'm getting from my Atlanta studio is that a lot of brides are buying the CD disk but are just putting it in their bank's safe deposit box.

Evidently someone started that trend and it's become a "thing" in Atlanta.

And it's really the case.

Some of these brides that already ordered the Hi-Res Disk have already ordered reprints.

Pretty much they don't want to deal with the hassle of printing, collating and sending out prints to family members.

Finally, not all products have to bring in money.

Some things you can do just to add value to what you're doing.

Right now, my studio will post a bride's wedding online as a courtesy.

We only do this on request, but it doesn't cost the bride anything.

Basically, after they get their proofs (but before they select their final album)—we'll post their pictures online.

We wait until they get their proofs first, so they will be the first one to see their wedding.

But after that, we put their wedding up on a password protected link.

At one time we discussed charging for this service. But since then, we decided to do it free or upon request.

The reason being is that it helps for us to get reprint orders. Another reason is that it drives people to my website.

I may charge for this service in the future, but right now things are fine the way they are.

The "Interview" with the Bride

Before a bride books with a studio, most will interview at least two or three potential photographers.

If you even get a call from a bride, know that's a good sign.

You at least made the final cut.

Chances are, they saw you somewhere or they had a friend that had you shoot their weddign.

So go into this meeting with confidence.

In places we don't have a physical studio; we meet them in a coffee shop.

Many weddings have been booked at Starbucks.

The beauty of being a wedding photographer is that you don't necessarily need to have a photo studio where you live.

There is no shame in being a home-based photographer.

Just about all of us were at one time in our career. And that includes myself.

One of my first professional photo shoots was in my ghetto-ridden apartment.

In fact, sometimes getting a studio too early in your career makes you look silly.

I know one photographer who has a day job, but rents a huge studio.

It sits empty all the time.

On the other hand, I know of photographers that are very successful and they work out of their home.

Having a physical studio isn't as important as it used to be.

Having a great website is.

Having a great reputation is.

And I would say that most of the "trust issues" of a photographer not having a physical studio is put to rest by having the ability to take major credit cards.

Whatever you do, don't let the photographers that do have physical studios bully you into thinking that somehow you're not a player.

It's important, but not that important.

So here you are.

You're meeting with the bride.

Bring with you two or three show books.

One is probably too little and four starts to be too much.

Have with you a copy of your wedding contracts (more on this later) and your rate cards.

Here is your objective.

You are here to show off your photography and you are there to make the bride feel comfortable.

Showing the photography off is the easy part.

Making the bride feel comfortable is the hard part.

Usually after the initial pleasantries, I offer the bride a chance to take a look at my work.

From here, it's just a matter of me keeping my mouth shut until she can look through my show books.

Along the way, I find out where the bride is having her wedding and reception.

If there are any pictures of either location in my books, I'll point them out.

And I usually only give "play by play" comments on my pictures if they ask about them.

And most of the time they will.

They ask where this or that picture was taken.

So having a great memory is a plus.

During this meeting, the bride is asking herself two questions:

Do I like these photos?

Do I feel comfortable having this person (you) around during my wedding day?

The fact of the matter is not everyone is going to book you. So relax.

Sometimes a bride doesn't book because they can actually sense that your personality is too assertive.

Maybe your confidence is coming off as arrogance.

Or maybe she doesn't book you because you're not assertive enough.

Maybe she has a family member that she can't control and needs someone to just take over.

You never know.

But nothing beats just being you and letting the chips fall where they may.

But what will help is your ability to know your craft.

The bride will come up with some questions that she might not even know the right answer to.

They do a lot of research. And sometimes they read somewhere that they need to ask a particular question.

So they do.

It's usually something like, "Do you use strobes or ambient lighting."

Hey … we know what that means. But she might not.

She just might have read it somewhere that you should ask that question.

So exude confidence and tell her.

She's probably more interested in how you react to the question than how you answer it.

But more than that, she will probably ask you a lot of questions on how you run your wedding packages.

For me, it's pretty easy.

This is what I say …

"Basically we have four different packages and they come with three things. The wedding time, your proofs and an album. The Elite package comes with the 5x7 album and the Heritage and above comes with the 8x10 album. And pretty much the higher packages come with more of the extras."

Now how simple is that?

In about one minute I just summed up my whole wedding operation.

From there, I just have to field questions.

Common questions are things like:

"When does the time start?"

"When do I get my pictures back?"

"Can I substitute things from the packages?"

On a rare occasion the bride will ask more personal questions. And she has a right to. This is in effect, a job interview.

Some of those questions include:

"How long have you been a photographer?"

"How many weddings have you photographed?"

"Have you ever shot in this church?"

Answer them honestly and with conviction.

My studio has a tremendous booking rate.

But when the brides book us, only about half fill out the contract and put down the deposit right there and then.

It isn't a secret that it's the bride that makes the decision on who to book.

We all know this. The groom? Well, he has little or almost no input on this.

But in a show of mock humility, the bride will usually wait until after the meeting to get her boyfriend's opinion.

Trust me, this is highly symbolic.

If the bride likes you, she's going to book you.

But bring along a wedding contract for them to look over and sign just in case.

The one I use is very simple.

Because two people are signing it, it is a legal document and a contract.

But in reality it's just a form we used to keep track of what's going on.

The bride fills out all the pertinent information:

Name, address, cell-phone number, where the wedding is and when.

We even have a spot for an email address.

From there, we take a retainer.

Notice that I called this a retainer and not a deposit.

Deposits by law are refundable. Retainers are not.

This is important that it's non-refundable because we're making a commitment to be there.

And once we sign this contract, then we pretty much have one less photographer that I can book.

The retainer amount I have used for years is $300.

Some photographers do more. Some less.

But over the years, I have felt very comfortable with this amount.

From there, we take that $300 off the package and the balance is due the Monday before the wedding.

Once I have a signed contract and the retainer in my hand, the bride is considered booked.

I give the bride a copy. I put the original contract in a fire-proof safe in my studio. And I make one more copy for my home office.

I also enter the wedding day on my online calendar.

From there, life is good.

Another wedding is in the books.

Preparation for the Big Day

You would think that once you sign the contract, that you wouldn't have conversations with the bride until the wedding day.

That is furthest from the truth.

On an average, there will be about 6 to 8 months time between your first meeting with her and the wedding date.

During this time, you will play a big role.

My preferred way of contact with the bride is through email.

Through that time period, I try to stay as active as possible with her.

A lot of times, they need some advice.

Where are they to go for the flowers?

Where to go for a limousine?

Does this videographer suck?

Here's your chance to shine.

Your input means everything to her.

Be prepared to make suggestions.

A lot of times, it's not just a referral they are looking for. Sometimes they want some good ideas.

Try to figure out your bride's personality and make suggestions as needed.

Maybe she's debating between throwing rose petals vs. blowing bubbles as they leave. You need to be prepared to have an opinion.

Over the years, I've become great friends with some of my brides.

It's this part of the wedding process that I love the most.

I have one friend who I found out that we have the same taste in comedies.

We're "Curb Your Enthusiasm" fans.

The months leading up to the wedding, we even started text messaging each other on funny episodes we remember.

During this time, your brides might also need some photos.

Two come to mind. The engagement photo and the bridal portrait.

Let me explain both.

The engagement photo is pretty self explanatory.

Your bride might need the photo for an announcement in the newspaper.

She also might want to display a picture at the reception.

It has become more and more popular to have what is called an "engagement signing board" at the wedding.

This is a blown up picture, usually 11x14, with an oversized mat around it.

Instead of signing a guest book, guests sign the mat.

There are other variations of this. We offer an engagment signing book where people do the same thing, but in an album format of their engagement shoot.

Either way, the bride might want an engagement sitting.

For the most part, our studio does these pictures complimentary.

We do the shoot and they pay for whatever they want and use.

If they just want a 5x7 picture for the newspaper—that's fine.

We're not really after money as much as we are using this opportunity to build a relationship.

When I do shoot and engagment, I usually go all out.

I take the couple to the beach or a park.

I take them in different settings. I get close-ups of the engagement ring.

I get pictures of them strolling along hand in hand.

It's fun. And it's an exciting time in their life.

However, if you live in the South, there is another product that is very popular.

It's called a bridal portrait.

I know some of our brides from the northern states don't know what this is.

But let me explain first what it is and then I will go on record on with my opinion.

The bridal portrait is a Southern Tradition.

It's when the bride puts on her bridal dress maybe two months before the wedding.

She comes into the studio or on location and the photographer takes her picture.

In turn, the bride takes this picture and displays it at the reception.

I include this service in some of my bigger packages. Other brides order this service "a la carte" and pay in the $300–$500 range to have this photo displayed at the reception.

Ok ... I'm coming from all angles here.

I have my foot in just about every part of the country.

I've was born in Brooklyn, New York.

I live in Myrtle Beach, South Carolina.

And I have studios all way west to Reno, Nevada.

I know the prejudice that people have about Southerners.

And the fact that bridal portraits aren't done up North is understandable.

For the most part, the South lags behind the North.

Fashion usually filters down from New York and then to the rest of the country.

Fads usually filter in from California and then onward.

But when it comes to weddings, the South rules.

The top two wedding destinations in the United States are Las Vegas first and then Charleston, South Carolina second.

You take into consideration that while Las Vegas has more than their share of glitz and glam weddings—it's also the capital of the quick and small weddings.

It's popular to elope in Las Vegas and or Reno.

But when it comes to the big event weddings … Charleston, SC and the south runs the show.

When it comes to wedding fads, they almost always start from the South and move onward.

You name it.

Butterfly releases. Groom Cakes. Bubble blowing.

These are all things that started in the South.

People travel to these destination weddings and then take these cool ideas and try them back home.

So when it comes to bridal portraits, you may or may not want to add them to your stable of products. But at least respect it and understand it.

I love them.

It gives me a chance to have a "dress rehearsal" with the bride.

And it gives me a chance to have a picture that I can show off at the wedding.

If you're asked to photograph a bridal picture—that's a good thing.

It's a chance to showcase your talent.

The Count Down

This is going to probably be the shortest chapter in the book. But it's also one of the most important.

No earlier than two weeks before the wedding and no later than the Monday before the wedding—I give my bride one more call.

This is so important.

Actually it never ceases to amaze me on how many last minute changes there are.

There have actually been times where the bride changed the location of the wedding during the weeks leading up to the wedding.

Granted, I need to know. But sometimes their head is so busy with things that they forget to call me.

That's ok. Your bride has a lot of things on her mind.

So call her a week before the wedding.

And touch base.

This is what I do.

You call up and have your wedding confirmation in hand.

And what you do is just go down that list to make sure that everything is still the same.

Of utmost importance is the place and time of arrival.

Usually, I like to be at a wedding an hour and a half before the actual start time.

That's because I like to get settled in. And if possible, I like to get some shooting done before the actual wedding.

I'll talk about this in the next chapter.

But ideally, I like to get pictures of the bride with her bridesmaids before the wedding.

This is usually an hour and a half before the wedding.

Then I like to get pictures of the groom with his groomsmen an hour before the wedding.

This leaves us a half hour of "chill time" before the wedding.

These are the things I discuss with the bride during this phone call or meeting.

Sometimes the logistics of the wedding don't allow for the above scenario.

That's fine. I work around whatever.

But at least touch base and figure it all out.

I also go over last minute specifics.

In particular, I ask if there is any situation that I should know about.

Are the parents divorced?

Is there going to be an awkward situation?

I also ask if there are any pictures that we need to get.

I'll talk about photo lists in the next chapter.

But the way I do it is much faster and much more effective than having a list around.

However, if there is a list—I need to know about it.

Or if someone is traveling in from a far distance and they need a photo of that person—I need to know about it.

Finally, I make sure that they are paid in full.

I take checks, cash and credit cards.

This is stated in the contract they signed way back when.

And it's non-negotiable.

I need to be paid in full before the wedding because I've seen everything.

I've seen people cancel the day of the wedding.

I've seen people get in a fight on the dance floor and split.

I've seen people run out of money.

I've seen wedding planners that "spent my money" and had nothing left to "pay me" with.

You have no idea.

So I've made a very reasonable rule.

I need, please, the payment in full, the Monday before the wedding.

The Wedding Day

Here we go.

This is the big day for both the bride and you.

I have a pretty good wedding day routine.

I make sure my morning is clear and I sleep in until maybe 10 am or so.

On any other day, I'm usually up by 8 am feeding my wiener dogs and getting ready for the day.

So I sleep in a little and then eat some food.

By 11 am or so, I go back to sleep.

Most of the time, I need to leave my home by 2 or 3 pm. So like to get as much rest as possible.

The way I figure it … my whole career is based on 5 or 6 hours of flawless work every Saturday.

I need to be at 100 percent every single weekend.

One of my friends is Jeremy Mayfield.

You might recognize his name.

He is one of the top drivers in the NASCAR racing circuit.

I did his wedding several years back when he married Myrtle Beach native Shana Sessions.

Ever since that wedding, we've been friends.

When the races come to Atlanta, Charlotte or the famed Darlington, South Carolina, I like to go.

I hang out with Shana and her parents.

But I hardly ever see Jeremy before the race.

Most of the time, he has things to do with his sponsors.

But usually before the race he's in his million-dollar RV sleeping with an oxygen tank.

How do you drive 190 mph for 4 hours straight?

I'm not sure. And I don't think I want to find out.

But I do know Jeremy has figured it out.

If taking a nap with oxygen gets him prepared—then that's what he needs to do.

For me, I need to be 100 percent at every wedding.

My career, reputation and my bride depend on it.

So my routine is to sleep in until 10 am. Eat a big meal. And then go back to bed until I'm ready to leave the house.

Sometimes I'm not at home. Sometimes I'm on the road doing a wedding.

But the same thing applies.

I get as much rest as possible.

Again, I have to be flawless for a 5-hour time frame.

So I do what I need to do.

The First Hour: I'm usually the second one at the wedding.

By this time, the florist has already made his or her way into the church or venue.

The first thing I do is get settled in.

I find a place to put my equipment.

So you know … this is what I have in my bag.

I go to the weddings with two cameras.

Both are Nikon digital cameras.

One camera has an 85mm F1.8 lens.

I use this for all my individual portraits and my general "all purpose" lens.

The other camera has a 50mm F1.8 lens.

I use this for my group photos.

My third lens is a 15mm fish-eye lens that I use sporadically during the wedding to add drama to the wedding.

That's it.

I have a Nikon flash that I use.

But primarily I shoot everything with available light.

I keep both cameras on my shoulders at all times.

I keep my flash, my fish-eye and my batteries, re-chargers, etc in my bag.

I make sure that at all times I know exactly where my cameras are.

A stolen camera I can replace.

A stolen camera with the wedding on the compact flash I can't.

I start my day by finding a place to keep my bag.

From there, I do a once over of the church or venue.

What I'm looking for is different places that I can shoot the pictures.

I make mental notes on different places.

I also take test shots of the different areas.

I take my meter readings and check my white balance in each area.

If need be, I ask my assistant for suggestions.

I try to take this in two steps.

For one, I try to find a nice place to take all the formal pictures.

Most of the time, this is nothing more than taking the wedding party or the families in front of the church.

In fact, that's what I do most of the time.

But to add an extra touch to the wedding, I always try to find a place where I can take the couple.

Most of the time, I try to find something outdoors.

My strategy here is to find something white.

The bride with a white accent to it is stunning.

It shouldn't be too hard to find this.

Most churches have some sort of white outside. Be it the white columns or maybe it's a white fence.

It's not a rule, just a nice starting place.

From there, I make a mental note on all the "cool" places I'll shoot the bride in later on.

This whole process takes about 15 minutes or so.

By now … I have about another 15 minutes or so to relax before my first shoot.

Next I try to find someone in charge.

Sometimes it's the mother of the bride.

Other times it's the wedding director.

Sometimes it's the bride herself.

What I basically do is just check in.

Hey … *"I'm here. I'm ready to work. I'm waiting for you."*

In a perfect world, I like to shoot the bride and her friends first.

Then I like to shoot the guys and his friends second.

For the sake of example, let's just assume that now …

Granted, each wedding is different. But let's just go with this scenario for now and you can make adjustments as necessary.

Ok … here we go.

After checking in, I find the wedding program.

Meet your best friend.

While waiting for the girls to come out, I take some time to study this program.

It's all you need to know.

It'll list everything you need to know.

The name of the maid of honor.

The name of the best man.

Everything.

Take a few minutes to study this.

My memory isn't the best in the world.

But at the very minimum, I try to remember the name of the maid of honor.

She will help you get through your day.

Know her name. Love her.

She will make your day smooth.

I also glance at the parents names.

Here I try to see if there's anything I need to know.

Granted I just asked her a week ago, but I try to determine once again if there's anything that could potentially be embarrassing to me.

Sometimes the parents are divorced and you can figure that out very quickly from the wedding program.

Sometimes a parent is deceased.

You can also determine this from the program.

I study it and make mental notes from it.

The next thing I do is take a picture of the program.

So you got that.

Now the fun begins.

At this time, I then start to take a picture of just about anything I can think of.

I call this "painting the room."

I take pictures of the little flowers on the altar.

I take pictures of the guest book.

I take pictures of the box of tissues where the mother of the bride sits.

I try to capture as much of the "mood" of the wedding as possible.

After this, I find the bride and get a few pictures of her getting ready.

Again, the first order of business is now to "paint the bride."

I take pictures of everything remotely connected to her.

I take a close-up picture of her shoes.

The back of her dress.

The detail on the hem of her dress.

At this time, I try not to disturb the bride. I kind of just sit back and watch the day unfold.

Granted I might want to get that mirror shot. But for the most part, I'm still in the background.

I take whatever goes on.

If her mother is putting on her veil, I take that.

If her maid of honor is putting on her garter, I get that.

When I'm finish, I make an announcement.

"Ladies. When you're finished, please meet me in the front of the church so we can take some pictures."

Now we are ready to begin the hard part.

The Formals: I know how some of you think about the old boring formal pictures.

Formal pictures are so boring.

I'm a photojournalist. Or I'm a candid photographer.

So great. Good for you.

But if you want to be a wedding photographer, you're going to have to learn to take the formal pictures.

No matter how modern your bride is or how alternative she is—she or her family will want some formal pictures of the family.

Yes.

They are going to stand there, look straight into your camera and smile.

Get used to it.

I know it's not the most enjoyable thing in the world.

I know you don't "feel" like an artist when you're doing it.

But learn to love it.

Once you get the hang of it, it can be fulfilling.

For the most part, everyone in the wedding party already has a bad attitude about these pictures.

That's because they've been tortured by other photographers. They stand in place for what seems like hours. They wait forever for their turn.

It doesn't have to be like that.

There's actually a science to it to make it go quickly and efficiently.

Let's start with the bride's side.

Bride Side Formals: **By now, the groom has been safely tucked away.**

Part of that is your responsibility.

The tradition is still alive today. This is the tradition where the bride and groom don't see each other before the actual wedding.

There are exceptions, but for the most part that's how it's done.

Just check to make sure the groom isn't around when the ladies come to the front of the church.

Ok … very simple.

Start with the bride with each one of her bridesmaids individually.

Basically, park the bride in the middle of the stage and shuffle her friends one at time to get their picture taken with her.

Angle them in towards each other, let them smile and shoot away.

Don't forget the once over for any picture.

Just glance around to make sure everything is in place.

In the days of old, this was painstaking because there wasn't any Photoshop correction.

Granted, you can be a little more lenient today, but you still have to watch out for stuff like things in the background or a necklace that's crooked.

When you're done, line up the bride with all her bridesmaids and do one group picture.

Save yourself a headache later and shoot multiple pictures of every formal.

Granted, for me to say "just line them up and shoot them" is easier said than done.

But it needs to be done and you can be as creative as you want with these shots.

There are many variations.

But for the most part, put the bride in the middle. Half the girls on one side, half on the other side.

It's not rocket science.

If it's an odd number, angle the bride and her maid of honor in the middle. Then put half on one side and then half on the other side.

Keep them there and add in the flower girl if they have one.

I always try to take at least one picture without the flower girl in it.

I'm just playing the odds here.

Most of the time, if the picture is screwed up, it's because there's a young girl in the picture who can't sit still or won't look into the camera.

The same principle goes with the ring bearer.

From here ... dismiss everyone except for the bride.

Now it's "repeat and rinse" again.

Same thing.

Bride with each family member.

One with just the mom.

Just the dad.

Just the sister.

If the bride's mom and dad are together—one with both of them.

If not … one with each of them with their current mates.

Save yourself from the wrath of the MOB.

Yes … the MOB.

The Mother of the Bride.

Other than the bride. Cater to the mom first.

It's a good rule. She's the queen bee.

Think of her needs first.

For example, never call up the father and his new wife to do pictures before you take care of the mother of the bride's pictures.

Bride.

Bride's Mom.

The President of the United States.

You got it?

That's the order of things.

Be sure to get one picture with all the immediate family (or it may be two sets if their parents have separated) and you're done.

As a note, I have a pretty simple rule.

If the bride has her new husband with her, then I ask the other people like the sisters and brothers to also bring their mate into the picture.

But if it's before the wedding, usually the bride doesn't have her groom with her.

So when I call up a picture of the bride with her sister—I don't call up her sister's husband to join them in the photo.

In essence, you get one picture with just her and her sister by themselves.

Later on, I'll get that picture.

And later on, I'll get the other pictures with the extended family.

Usually I also save grandparents till later as well.

Now you have one more thing to do.

Dismiss everyone except for the bride and her maid of honor.

You still have to get some pictures of the bride by herself.

But keep the maid of honor nearby.

She will help you with these next photos.

She will help relax your bride and she knows all the tricks to do that.

She is your friend. Love the maid of honor.

God said, "Do not covet thy neighbor's wife."

But he never did say anything about the Maid of Honor.

Ok … bad joke.

Funny, but bad.

Ok … from here, you're just doing a nice 10 minute photo shoot with the bride.

Take her outside. Take her to different "cool" places around the church.

Do your thing.

Take several pictures of the bride by herself—full length.

Take some pictures of her from the waist up.

Have her looking into the camera. Have her looking away.

Have her looking down at her flowers.

This doesn't have to be a major production. Just get some pictures of her looking good.

Once you finish this, the bride's side is done.

The bride goes back to seclusion and we get out the groom.

The Groom Side Formals: Have you noticed a pattern yet?

It's the same thing over again … this time it's with the groom's side.

I call it "rinse and repeat."

The other pattern is that I'm building my pictures from small to big.

I start out with "small" individuals and or groups. And then I go "big" by adding people into the pictures.

Groom with groomsmen.

All the groomsmen together.

All the groomsmen with the ring bearer.

All the groomsmen with the ring bearer and the ushers.

Small to Big.

Then with the family pictures.

Small to Big.

Groom with individual family member, Groom with all family members.

The groom pictures are always fun.

Anytime you have that much testosterone in the same room, the guys always have to give the groom a hard time.

There's a lot of teasing and laughing.

It's all good. Let them have their fun.

But be firm. Don't let one jerk guy in the wedding party mess up your pictures.

Again, I've seen it all.

I had one groomsmen drop his tuxedo pants down to his ankles for the formal pictures.

Ok ... ha ha. I get it. You're a funny guy.

Take one picture like that. Humor him.

And then tell him to put his pants back up and get back to your job.

Don't let one guy ruin your pictures.

When you're done with the groom/groom's men pictures and the groom with his immediate family, you have one more thing to do.

Get a few good pictures of the groom by himself.

Take him outside. Get a few pictures of him looking into the camera.

Get a few pictures of him looking away.

And you're done.

I try to get this all done so I have a half hour of rest time before the actual wedding.

You will need it.

The Actual Wedding: The half hour leading up to the wedding is for you to gather your thoughts.

Sometimes I just sit and think about different angles I can shoot from.

Most of the time, my choices are limited.

That's because there are rules and you need to find out what they are.

I usually hunt down whoever is doing the ceremony and ask him or her for the church's "ground rules."

By far, the most frequent rule I run into is "no flash photography."

The next most popular rule is "shooting only from the back."

On a rare occasion they will have a "no photography" rule at all.

If they go to that extreme, I always cover my bases by telling the bride what the preacher said.

If that is the case, you just have to do your best.

Usually, I hang out in the lobby of the church and try to get as many pictures as I can as the wedding party is standing around waiting to enter.

I know it's not fair and especially when they have such harsh rules for professionals.

I mean, just about anyone with a point and shoot can flash away from the pews, but you get shut out.

But it's what it is.

A lot of times you can "negotiate" with the preacher.

Sometimes you can clarify the "no photographs" rule.

Sometimes they say the ceremony STARTS when the bride makes it to front and ENDS when the preacher announces them husband and wife.

If that is the case, then at least you can get the pictures of the wedding party coming in and going out.

And in a best case scenario, the first kiss.

Do your best under the circumstance.

But if there are no rules, keep in mind to be respectful.

Assuming that you're allowed free reign in the church, keep in mind not to be a distraction.

You want to avoid becoming part of a circus.

So I usually park myself on an aisle seat in the middle of the church.

Usually when something happens … I crouch down in the middle of the aisle and take my shot.

Most of the time, I wait until there's some music or some singing going on. This prevents the clicking of my camera from being overwhelming.

In a nutshell, get everything that goes on.

If they light candles, get it.

If they kneel down, get it.

If a friend is giving a scripture reading, then get that as well.

If I'm able to, I'll discreetly go over to the front and get pictures of the parents sitting at the pews.

But if you're close to the end of the ceremony, go back to the center aisle and try to get the first kiss.

As much as you would think it would be an issue, it's not the end of the world if you miss this shot.

In fact, don't panic at all.

It's easy to be thrown off your game.

Don't worry. The whole is greater than the sum of its parts.

Just go out there and get great pictures.

When the wedding is over, the wedding party walks up the aisle.

Make sure you get plenty of these pictures.

And when they finish, someone will come down and usher the parents up the aisle.

Again … make sure you get plenty of these photos because you're going to get a lot of out of focus pictures.

Some photographers ask the wedding party members to stop so they can get a picture of them.

Not that that's a bad thing, but I'd rather not do that.

I'd rather stay as much in the background as possible during a wedding.

If you know or think you missed a photo of someone coming up the aisle—don't panic.

You can get them outside the church hugging the bride or shaking hands with the groom.

Taking wedding photos isn't like taking a wedding video.

With video, you have to make sure you know what's going on every second in order not to miss anything.

Some photographers like to restage pictures that they missed or they were not allowed to photograph.

While I'm not above that, I'd rather take a real artistic picture of say the unity candle or the first kiss.

If I missed that, then so be it.

But if the bride is handing a rose to her mother during the ceremony and I miss it … I have a back-up plan.

In that case, I will take a close-up picture of that rose later on.

I do want to appear as candid and true as possible, but in this case, art triumphs over truth.

I'll get what I can and when I can.

At the same time, I don't blame you if you want to restage a picture.

Moving on …

From this point, the bride and groom should be isolated from the guests.

In a perfect world, the wedding guests are asked to go straight to the reception.

But other times, the bride chooses to have a reception line.

Reception lines make for a long day.

If the bride and groom take a half hour greeting guests outside the church, then it will usually be at least an hour and half before the reception begins.

Not that you have a say in it, but if asked—always try to discourage any kind of reception line.

It's better to have the guests leave and the bride and groom go into temporary "hiding."

Once the church is cleared out of guests, you're ready to begin your last set of formal photos.

We're almost finished.

After Ceremony Formals: **Ok … do you remember how we did it before?**

It's the same thing.

That's right.

Small to Big. Rinse and Repeat.

Here we go ...

Just one exception after the ceremony.

I usually like to get the bride and groom with the preacher first.

It's a nice courtesy for the preacher so he doesn't have to sit there and wait.

After that, you're ready to go.

Ok ... bride's side first ...

Mom and Dad with Bride and Groom.

Add in grandparents.

Add brothers and sisters with their mates and children.

Add in all other extended relatives.

The brides side is done.

Then the groom's side goes next.

Same thing. Small to Big.

Mom and Dad with Bride and Groom.

Add in Grandparents.

Add in brothers and sisters with their mates and children.

Add in all other extended relatives.

The groom's side is done.

It really is that simple.

Now there are just two more things you have to do.

The first is one picture with the whole wedding party.

The simplest way by far is to make an announcement.

"Ok … wedding party, please. Line up on the stage the same exact way you did during the wedding."

From there, the wedding party coaches themselves into their position.

Wow … what a time saver.

Now all you have to do is "tighten up" the shot a little and take the photo.

You are done.

From here, whisper to the bride and groom and say this …

"We're done with the entire formal pictures except for you two. Before I let everyone go, are there any other pictures we need of anyone here?"

Please say this.

It will make your life so much easier later on.

Just ask them if there's anything else.

Usually, they will have one or two simple requests.

Most of the time, they want a picture with a girlfriend and her husband. Or maybe it's a cousin that they want an individual picture with.

Get that.

Then from there, dismiss everyone one from the church except the bride, groom and maid of honor.

From here, take some pictures of the couple together.

I usually like to take them outside for a 15 minute shoot.

Or, I'll take them to different parts of the church that I found interesting.

Either that or I might do some inside the church and then take the rest at the reception hall.

It just depends.

But get plenty of pictures of this.

The combinations are plentiful.

Full length of the bride and groom.

Waist up.

Looking at each other.

Kissing.

Holding hands.

Kissing each other on the cheek.

What you do is entirely up to you. But have fun.

This is the best part of the wedding.

By now you should be totally at ease.

Your bride is relieved that the wedding is finished.

You're relieved that the formals are done.

You could just have fun now.

The Reception

By the time you make it to this point, the day is going well.

Now you can relax and hang out in the background.

Start by "painting the reception room."

You remember.

This is the same technique you did at the church and with the bride.

Take detail pictures of everything.

Take pictures of the cake, the table settings, and the little bow behind the chairs.

Take pictures of the candles, the flowers on the table and the ice sculpture.

Next, touch base with who will be your best friend for the next two hours.

You have abandoned the maid of honor.

You now have a new best friend.

It will be the DJ.

Or sometimes it's the wedding director.

But someone there will know exactly what's going to take place. And that person will be your best friend.

Someone will be calling the shots when these things will take place.

And you need to know when and where.

These must have shots are:

> The First Dance
>
> The Cake Cutting
>
> The Dance with the Father of the Bride
>
> The Toast
>
> Best Man's Speech

Not all brides choose to have all these events, but it's hard to find a wedding without a majority of these things.

There is more.

In some Northern weddings, it's a custom for the new couple to visit each table and toast them.

If they do that, then it's the photographer's responsibility to follow them around at this time and get a picture of each table.

I know that's not that fun, but if it's your job then that's what you need to do.

Other than that, your main job at this point is to get fantastic candid pictures.

Spend 80 percent of your time at this shooting 20 percent of the people.

While you want to get good pictures of the guests, concentrate your energies on family members and members of the wedding party.

The wedding party people are easy.

But be on the lookout for the family members.

I call them "the people of the flower."

They are the ones that got pinned with a flower earlier in the day.

If they walk out on the dance floor, you follow them.

If the bride is dancing and they are laughing, you turn around and photograph them.

Remember. Get the most important people at the reception.

You will know who they are.

Have fun and do your job until the evening draws to a close.

And when it does, there is more work to do.

Some couples plan an elaborate leave.

Throwing rice really isn't done anymore.

They have been replaced with more eco-friendly rose petals or bird seed.

Rose petals decay and birds eat the seeds.

On the other hand, birds don't eat up the rice.

There are other options.

Some couples also have guest blow bubbles or light sparklers.

Oye.

I hate sparklers.

I hate being on fire.

I just think it's a bad idea to give fire to drunken people.

Just my opinion.

Either way, find a nice place to stand and shoot away.

Look for opportunities.

If they are leaving in a limo, ask the driver if you can photograph them from the passenger seat in the front.

From there you can take a picture of the couple through the divider window.

Work hard and you will know when you're done.

Congratulations!

You have just finished another successful wedding.

You're done.

Just one more thing …

Before you leave, just double check that you have all your equipment.

But again, that is a relative statement.

You shouldn't have to worry about where your camera is because it should always be on your shoulder.

I shoot everything on two compact flash cards.

I keep one in each camera.

I do that because I never have to worry about misplacing a card.

But if you switched out anytime during the night, make sure you have everything before you leave.

And even after you leave, you're not quite finished yet.

Once you get home, the first order of business will be to download your cards and burn them onto a CD.

I make three copies. Two go to my studio. And one stays in my home.

Technically at this point, I actually have five copies of the wedding. I usually wait until Monday morning to erase the cards on my compact flash.

So that is copy four.

And of course, I also have one copy on my laptop.

That is copy five.

And I am generally not a morbid person. But if I'm traveling on an airplane—I'll take one of the burned discs and mail it to myself.

Just a thing I do.

ee

After that, I relax.

And when you get to that point, you can too.

Good job.

The Week After

Back in the day ... and this was in the world of film and the days of Fred Flintstone ... life was actually easier.

You would pack up your film, and send it off to the best developer you could find.

But things aren't like that anymore.

Sounds crazy, but things actually got harder.

Now that responsibility of developing photos has been taken out of the developer's hand and put into yours.

Back in the day, it used to be that they were one-half of the battle.

You would shoot the wedding and your developer would compensate for all your errors.

They would crop it right.

They would correct your exposures.

They would make sure the color balance was perfect.

At that time, the skilled film processor was very much in demand.

That's not the case anymore.

As you know, today when we shoot, we fix the picture in Photoshop.

We do all the work the "developer" used to do.

We crop.

We correct exposures.

We color balance.

Now we do that.

And all that is left is to find best output service.

On a side note, I thought it was interesting what some of the strategies the film developers have adopted to survive.

One film developer I know is taking a unique strategy to compensate for their loss of work.

What they are doing now is offering a "raw developing" service.

Basically you give them a raw file, and then they process it, make all the color balance adjustments and crop it.

While I applaud their efforts to adjust to a new way of doing things, there is no way I would ever allow that for my photos.

I like full control of my vision.

When I finish a wedding, I like to do all the work to it.

I like to crop it myself. I like to correct my own white balance mistakes.

I like to decide for myself if the picture should be in black and white or not.

To hand over control of this to an outside source is pure laziness.

So the week following my wedding, I'm at the studio.

I start by taking each photo I took of the wedding and judge it for its worthiness.

Basically, I go through my wedding and throw out the crap.

And there will be a lot of junk.

On any given wedding, I shoot probably 600–800 photos.

Out of that, the bride and groom might get 350 or so photos.

Not everything will be perfect.

But I will tell you, the photos I give them will be perfect.

I feel good about this, because on my rate card, I promise them anywhere from 140 to 240 pictures.

The bride gets more than her baker's dozen.

So this is what I do …

I start by editing out all the bad pictures.

The pictures with the closed eyes.

The pictures where I just didn't get it right.

And sometimes I'll throw away a picture just because I have three or four picture of it that look just as good.

Either way … when it all comes down to the end, I have about 300 or so pictures to work with.

The next few days are spent taking these photos and "cleaning them up."

I take them and crop them right, make the necessary color balance adjustments and fix my mistakes.

I do take some pictures and convert them to black and white.

I will also take some pictures and leave everything but the flowers in color.

And while we're on the subject, I do want to make a point about this.

I was the first photographer to do this technique of taking a black and white photo and coloring in the flowers in wedding photography.

I know that a lot of photographers have criticized me saying to prove it. But I was the first one to introduce this in wedding photography.

I know this because I was one of the first wedding photographer to go digital.

Frankly, it's not a new idea. Photographers have been hand tinting black and white photography for ages.

But I did introduce this into modern wedding photography.

Ok … moving on.

So I take all my wedding pictures and I clean them up.

I get them processed and then I'm ready to give them to the bride.

And there, they have their complete project.

Delivering the Product

In my rate cards, I promise 4 to 6 weeks to get the wedding proofs back.

I also promise 6 to 8 weeks to get the album to them after they order it.

I crush these numbers.

Even in the busiest of months, I make sure that the bride gets their wedding proofs back in about 3 weeks.

Same goes for the albums.

Full disclosure ...

It wasn't always like that.

There was a time in my life, when even 8 weeks would have been a blessing.

There was a time in my life when I was very distracted with a bitter divorce.

At that time, it probably took 8 weeks to get the proofs to my brides.

And the albums?

Forget it.

Maybe 6 months.

It was just a rotten time in my life.

And to top it off, I had people working for me that weren't exactly after my best interests.

I couldn't get the albums out, because I just couldn't afford it.

At the time, with all the "mumbo jumbo" going on in my life, I was as close to bankrupt as possible.

I remember the day when I visited a bankruptcy lawyer.

Wow ... not good.

And not to smite people that had to go bankrupt, I am very happy to be able to say that I never had to go that route.

Those were dark days in my life.

But I learned so much from it.

Here's a tip for you.

When you get $2,000 from a bride—you don't keep $2,000.

Part of that goes to paying for the actual "product" that the bride gets.

It's going to be about 30 percent.

I know, because I already did the math.

Yes. I know.

It will be different for every photographer.

You will personally decide what you will charge the bride and what "products" you will give her.

But I'm telling you now, that it will come very close to 30 percent.

If it's less, that is fine.

If it's more, that is also good.

But it's going to come damn close to 30 percent.

And that's what you need to save.

The bottom line is this.

When you take $1,000 ... $1,000 does not belong to you.

In my estimations, maybe about $700 of it belongs to you.

That $300 has to go somewhere.

Using this system, you still owe your bride some "product."

And when it's time to deliver, you have to come up with the product.

If you're smart, you might take that $300 or so and invest it.

So by the time the bride asks for her album, you not only have it—but you have more than you need.

For me, I'm not that crafty.

I need to save that $300.

I take that money and put it in a special place.

I don't even keep it in a savings account.

I'm sure you're like me. If you see it there, you're going to want to spend it.

I take that money and in effect hide it.

And when the bride orders her album, the only thing slowing me up is the album company to produce it.

So that's how it's done.

When I get the bride her proofs, I also give her the order form she needs to "cash in" her wedding album.

I also give her order forms for parent albums and a special "Friends and Family" form.

If things work out, the bride will give me back her order with a big fat check she's collected from family members.

Yes ... life is good when you get paid for things you did way back when.

The Days and Years After

You know what you want.

You're basically hoping to do the wedding and pick up a client for life.

In a perfect world, you're also picking up a friend for life.

To this day, I'm personal friends with brides I photographed eight or nine years ago.

It's almost something that I never wanted to be.

When I first started 17 or 18 years ago, I despised the idea of becoming the "family photographer."

But now that I'm here, it's not so bad.

I like it when brides call me up four, five or six years after their wedding day to take pictures of their children.

I always swore that the day I photograph the wedding of the child, of the bride, I shot … is the last wedding I'll do.

When that day comes, who knows?

When I first started taking picture, I hated that family photographer.

I thought, "This is the guy that's getting all the work here. And what is he? He's out of touch. He doesn't understand what the modern bride wants."

And you know, maybe I was right.

I've seen many photographers come and go.

But the day I reach that milestone of photographing a second generation wedding, I would hope that the young bride actually wants to book me.

I don't want to rely on the "good word" of her mother—the bride I shot way back when.

I want to stay cutting edge.

I want the bride 10 years from now to hire me because I'm see things from a new perspective.

So that's what you need to do.

Here I included a modern day outline of how to photograph weddings.

Take this and run with it.

And when you do, you will open up new ideas.

And when you do, you will forge for yourself a career that you will cherish forever.

The Gene Ho Story

Thank you so much for taking the time to read this book.

I honestly hope that you can benefit from my ideas.

I hope you'll skip all the mistakes I've made and outlined in this book.

I hope you will expedite your career.

I changed so much over the years.

When I first started shooting photos, it was all about me.

All I cared about what was my bottom line.

But today, I've changed.

Today, the most important thing to me now is the legacy.

Right now, the most important thing I can do is to connect with the new generation of hot-shot photographers.

And I'm with you.

I know. I've been there.

When I first started photography, I was a little arrogant.

Maybe that's a good thing.

I loved photography and wanted so bad to be on the top of my game.

I can't tell you how hard I worked.

I never cared about money or time. I just busted my ass ... every day.

But I just knew that if I worked hard, that I could make it.

Ok … one more confession.

I have photos of my first wedding portfolio in my junk drawer.

You know what I'm talking about.

The junk drawer.

In there is a couple aspirins.

There are a few old birthday cards.

But I also keep something very dear to me.

I keep the photos from my first wedding portfolio.

I have them there as a reminder.

It's a reminder of how much I used to blow.

I used to suck.

Those wedding photos were a joke.

But it's what it was.

You might just be starting out. Or you might be already there.

But I feel that if you just apply just part of the ideas I talked about—you could take your career to a whole other level.

Before I close out this book, I do want to give a little biography about myself.

From the beginning, I was a loser.

Imagine yourself playing second fiddle to your brother or sister.

My sister, Maggie, forged a path that no one could keep up with.

Name it.

My sister went to the Ivy League.

She went to medical school.

Today, she is a doctor.

And her husband … he is also a doctor.

My brother-in-law is bad ass.

He graduated in the top of his medical class.

The Ivy League "Cornell University" offered him a job teaching.

He declined.

Not enough money in teaching for him. Not even in the Ivy League.

So he went into private practice.

And today, my sister and my brother-in-law have a happy home with three beautiful children.

And they live on two medical doctor incomes.

But me?

I was a loser.

I graduated the bottom 2/3 percentile of my High School class.

I went to college and proceeded to drop out.

Here's the end all of it all.

If you love photography, you can make a career of it.

Photography is the only art where you can build upon passion alone.

I love sports.

I have double the passion of the average Sportscenter addict.

But I will never amount to anything as an athlete.

I don't care how much I try, there's just nothing there.

I also love music.

It would be a close second … but I do imagine myself as Bon Jovi every once in a while.

That would be a great career.

And I do have the passion for it.

I love music.

But there's only so far I can go. And believe me, it's not far.

But photography is an animal all on its own.

Here's the deal.

Have a passion for photography, and the rest will follow.

Don't worry about the money. Don't worry about the time you spend.

Work hard in photography and you will make it.

You can do it.

And perhaps wedding photography will be the way.

I'm sure it will if you please learn from my mistakes.

I've been there and back.

And I know that what I say here is the key to your future.

But in anything you do, know that passion is the key.

Have passion and the rest will follow.

978-0-595-44228-7
0-595-44228-5

www.ingramcontent.com/pod-product-compliance
Lightning Source LLC
Chambersburg PA
CBHW021544200526
45163CB00015B/1356